IAN KNOX trained as an architect at Heriot-Watt University, ~~Edinburgh, graduating with~~
a B. Arch (Hons) in 1968. After a number of years working ~~as~~
he moved to cartoon films and worked for Halas and Batc~~helor~~
(Montreal) and Icotopoulix (Toronto). He also drew for IPC ~~and~~
left-wing magazines including *Red Weekly* and *Socialist Chall~~enge~~*. ~~He has been the~~
News political cartoonist since 1989 and also draws cartoon~~s for~~
BBC Northern Ireland's award-winning *Hearts and Minds*.

Culture Vultures

**Political Cartoons
1990–1999**

Ian Knox

THE
BLACKSTAFF
PRESS

BELFAST

for Ulrike, Sara, Jim,
Mum and Dad

First published in 1999 by
The Blackstaff Press Limited
Blackstaff House, Wildflower Way, Apollo Road
Belfast BT12 6TA, Northern Ireland

Printed by The Guernsey Press Company Limited

A CIP catalogue record for this book
is available from the British Library

ISBN 0-85640-660-0

Contents

ACKNOWLEDGEMENTS

I would like to thank those who suggested this book, kept asking me when it was coming out and helped put it together. In particular, I would like to thank the staff at Blackstaff Press for painstaking efficiency and coffee, and Fionnuala O Connor, who wrote the foreword and who, with the Davids, helped me make the initial selection.

I am also grateful to current and former staff at the *Irish News*, especially Terry McGlaughlin, Nick Garbutt, Tom Collins, Noel Doran, Seamus Kelters, Billy Graham, Kathleen Bell, Steve O'Reilly, Steve McCaffery and Niall Blaney, who at various points stopped what they were doing to check various dates and quotations. Thanks also goes to the team at *Hearts and Minds*.

Others who helped in various ways were Cathal Tohill, Julian Watson, Pete Matthews, Sean Lennon, Harry Irwin, Geoff Lloynes, Andrew Keating, Terry Willers and all the cartoonists from Rathdrum and Skibbereen, Michael Howland, Brian and Maire, Tom and Ellen Breheny, Eric and Joanne Elliott, Ned Chambers and Jack Holland.

Foreword

Inside a short time, Ian Knox's cartoons have become a new and heartening feature of our landscape, instantly recognisable. At the least mention of their names, several leading political figures take shape in people's minds, not as they would like to be imagined but as Ian draws them. In one cartoon in the autumn of 1999, while others hurry into talks with George Mitchell, Gerry Adams and David Trimble slouch at the school gates like bad boys, sneakers untied, baseball caps on back to front. John Hume races inside with an apple for teacher. Ian Paisley roars from jaws strung with spluttering saliva, great teeth like a portcullis.

Most of our political figures are woefully familiar. Ian Knox refocuses tired eyes. We are lucky to have him, lucky that he is funny without the idle nastiness of others, never cynical or jaded. The fun is cream on top of sharp political commentary and striking draughtsmanship.

While this collection includes drawings from other newspapers, it concentrates on Ian Knox's ten years at the *Irish News*. A pocket cartoon on the *Irish News*'s front page, a first for Northern Ireland, came after a stint of weekly half-page spreads which have established public figures as a full cast of Knox characters. The front-page cartoon is now an integral part of the paper. Television exposure on BBC Northern Ireland's politics programme *Hearts and Minds* extends and reinforces his newsprint impact, the Knox style imprinted through trailers and opening credits to the folder of fresh sketches for each show.

Over and over he hits the target smack in the middle, wonderful drawing honed by acute perception. The essential David Trimble glimmers from a bespectacled beetroot. A morose John Hume mooches past. Mo Mowlam beams out of great folds of drapery. Bob McCartney, reduced to child-size and dressed as a girl, trustingly holds a towering Paisley's hand. The infant Jeffrey Donaldson makes fleeting appearances in his nappy. 'It's Ian's chins I like,' one veteran observer mused. 'Jeffrey Donaldson's little chin, trying to be tough and ending up as Junior MachoMan. John Taylor's magnificent chin, that curious extra chin of David Trimble's.'

Minor players are as exactly done as the big parts: busy Monica McWilliams, lip curled in disgust, a marvellous Nigel Dodds with clifflike jaw. Relationships leap off page and screen. A breathless David Trimble, cast as boxer, looks towards the corner of the ring and the shadowed face of his deputy, John Taylor, all dark eyes and jowls. 'Of course I'm prepared to fight my corner,' says Trimble. Thud goes the arrow, dead centre.

If Ian has a weakness, it might be the repetition of his least attractive images: knuckle-dragging bandsmen uncomfortably reminiscent of *Punch*'s nineteenth-century apelike Paddies, Paisley forever ranting. Unionists unmistakably take the brunt of his scorn. But a charge of distortion would be hard to sustain and the faces and flair are irresistible. For a political commentator, having Knox drawings as an illustration is richly rewarding, and always a challenge. Few could ever hope to catch the heart of the matter in words as he so unfailingly does with precisely observed expressions and quirks of face or behaviour.

Ian's hold on the public mind is above all remarkable, given that ten years ago he had no slot in the mainstream media. As Northern Ireland's most accessible, popular and most instantly recognisable artist, he succeeds the once ubiquitous Rowel Friers, equally distinctive, though a very different cartoonist. When Rowel died, Ian Knox wrote gracefully about the older man's strengths, under a drawing that caught both Rowel and himself and the spirit of his art. Rowel shied away from politics, Ian relishes it. In a period of often dismaying and difficult political development, we have found a complex cartoonist for this very complex age.

FIONNUALA O CONNOR
BELFAST
OCTOBER 1999

Preface

I grew up in a quiet part of Belfast in a quiet patch of history. I knew there had been 'troubles' in the past in the same way that I knew there had been dinosaurs and coal swamps, but sure, that kind of thing was over and done with. True, there were still things happening in other parts of the world but just as L.P. Hartley wrote that 'the past is a foreign country, they do things differently there', so it seemed reasonable to assume that foreign countries were living in the past and would soon be doing the same as us.

At school no one was interested in politics apart from the very odd young fogey, a type still readily available to television producers wishing to screen shows such as 'Tony Blair Meets Young People'.

Eventually it dawned on me that other people – Catholics – lived in Northern Ireland too. I'd always known they were around but hadn't seen too much of them. Suddenly there they were, living separate parallel lives amongst us, and none too happy about it. I was in Edinburgh studying to be an architect when news began to filter through of sit-downs, squats and stand-offs, not to mention civil rights. I gradually eased off architecture and became a lazy political junkie. If I had any unionist sensibilities up to this time, then the trauma of losing them has blotted out the memory.

From Edinburgh I headed to London, where I cut my teeth doing international cartoons for a leftie newspaper that described the Soviet Union as a deformed workers' state. The intellectual rigour imposed by cartooning dialectical materialism served as an ideal toughening-up process for later tackling that most thorny of subjects – the Irish answer.

Back in Belfast I phoned Terry McGlaughlin, acting editor of the *Irish News*, and made him an offer he could have refused but didn't. I've been here ever since.

Nearly all the cartoons in this collection appeared in the *Irish News* (one comes from the *Sunday Tribune* and a few were in *Ireland on Sunday*) and they deal with local issues. Since we're a microcosm of the world, that makes them pretty international. Don't read this in the shop. Buy it and take it home.

IAN KNOX
BELFAST
OCTOBER 1999

The Peace Process

My period at the *Irish News* corresponds roughly with that other memorable period of history known as the peace process. In hindsight we now know that though everyone was in secret contact with everyone else, not everybody felt comfortable about it. John Major claimed that the idea of secret talks, had they existed, would have made him sick. When it came out that not only did they exist but that he was a major player, he managed to look convincingly pale. The fact that the roof did not collapse with these revelations was due to the many other supports that were sustaining the process – indeed its complexity was its strength.

The peace process was the product of many converging influences, the Hume–Adams talks and Secretary of State Peter Brooke's historic announcement in 1990 that Britain had no 'selfish strategic or economic interest' in Northern Ireland being but two. More important, however, was the anonymous and dangerous work carried out by Father Alex Reid – and others – who established lines of communication between previously hostile groups.

Also about this time another perverse struggle was playing itself out – the war between Sinn Féin and the IRA. Each political bridgehead that the former appeared to establish in the Republic, the latter destroyed by a bomb somewhere else. The contradiction became obvious, even to the participants, and the great struggle was superseded by the great debate which resulted in the great flood of documents incorporating the word 'peace' in the title. Elsewhere violent loyalism, when it began to develop a political voice, produced communicators of such rationality and progressiveness that it seemed like an ultra-leftist's daydream.

Across the Atlantic another important influencer was coming into view: Bill Clinton, a man of many special relationships, none of them with John Major. British politicians did, of course, play their part – Tony Blair, Mo Mowlam, and now Peter Mandelson.

Ceasefires, cessations, deadlines, and helicopters on the lawn – we've had them all. Most people think they've helped. As Tony Blair might have said: 'It's getting better all the time . . . or at least not as bad as it was five years ago. . .'

John Hume's exhaustive efforts to draw Sinn Féin into an inclusive peace process are initially rejected but subsequently taken over by Dublin and London.

NOVEMBER 1993

In the run up to the Downing Street Declaration of December 1993 there is evidence of cross-community support for the revived Hume–Adams initiative. Not all are pleased.

NOVEMBER 1993

Though generally welcomed, the announcement of an IRA ceasefire on 31 August 1994 produces explosions of fury and prophecies of doom from predictable quarters.

SEPTEMBER 1994

The three main loyalist groups follow the IRA in declaring a ceasefire. The young clean-shaven and dark-spectacled Gerry Adams and a younger dark-spectacled Gusty Spence have evolved into middle-aged, pipe-smoking peace brokers.

OCTOBER 1994

Expectations for an increased period of parole for paramilitary prisoners at Christmas are dashed by Sir Patrick Mayhew. An angry Cardinal Cahal Daly insists that an exercise of imagination on this issue would produce dividends.

DECEMBER 1994

The much-hyped Framework Documents are met with general acceptance from nationalists and screaming hysteria from unionists when they are jointly launched in Belfast by Taoiseach John Bruton and Prime Minister John Major.

FEBRUARY 1995

Patrick Mayhew meets Sinn Féin at Stormont Castle and is loudly condemned by Ian Paisley, Ken Maginnis, Conor Cruise O'Brien and various right-wing Tories. Meanwhile, Gerry Adams, one year on from the announcement of the republican ceasefire, is under pressure from hardline republican activists to produce some evidence of political engagement from a British government they accuse of 'stretching the process to the limit'.

JULY 1995

In a speech at Queen's University Belfast Patrick Mayhew announces the restoration of 50 per cent remission for paramilitary prisoners. He also hints at a mysterious white paper 'this autumn' and a review of emergency legislation. An *Irish News* editorial 'finds difficulty' in seeing it as anything other than a 'holding exercise'.

AUGUST 1995

In February 1996 the IRA ceasefire ends with a bomb explosion at Canary Wharf in London. Later that same year, speculation mounts that Downing Street is about to announce news of a new IRA ceasefire. As Major, Hume and Adams engage in an intensive round of talks and diplomacy, reactions vary wildly.

NOVEMBER 1996

John Hume's efforts to deliver a Christmas ceasefire one year on from Bill Clinton's visit to Ireland are met with indifference from Downing Street.

NOVEMBER 1996

As scuffles break out in the queue for Gilmore's New Year electrical sale, Sinn Féin protest that deals were done to exclude them from talks.

DECEMBER 1996

John Hume delivers an ultimatum to Sinn Féin that he will 'look elsewhere' for a means of making progress if republicans fail to deliver a permanent ceasefire. Ruling out a pre-election pact, he warns nationalists that a vote for Sinn Féin would be a vote for 'the murder of innocent human beings'. Adams claims that the parties are still in touch.

FEBRUARY 1997

14

The DUP surprises many observers by pulling its candidates out of two highly marginal seats. Gerry Adams makes a 'last-minute appeal' to the SDLP for talks on electoral issues.

APRIL 1997

Despite assertions that bread-and-butter politics, crime and security are the real issues,
this general election is no different from previous ones in Northern Ireland.

APRIL 1997

Two months into his premiership, Tony Blair spells out his visions for peace
in the House of Commons. Mo Mowlam offers to chair proximity talks between
Orangemen and Garvaghy Road residents at Hillsborough Castle.

JUNE 1997

After the restoration of the IRA ceasefire in July 1997 . . .

Will they or won't they meet for talks? All sides indulge in eleventh-hour displays of posturing and sparring. Sinn Féin surprises everyone by quickly signing up to the Mitchell Principles. Wrong-footed, the Ulster Unionist Council executive hastily gathers to decide on its participation.

SEPTEMBER 1997

18

Sure you know Stormont
– their tables have to be
different!

SEPTEMBER 1997

DECEMBER 1997

FEBRUARY 1999

Speakers at an international medical conference at the Waterfront Hall warn
of the health dangers lurking in the restricted Northern Irish diet.

Mo Mowlam appeals to the DUP and the UKUP to return to the talks. They respond
by launching a series of anti-talks rallies and demanding a referendum on the Union.

SEPTEMBER 1997

Tony Blair drives participants in the talks process to agree key issues
before Christmas.

DECEMBER 1997

Various venues are touted for the coming talks, notably an isolated Castle Endgame in Wales where parties will be cut off outside contacts. Comparisons with Michael Collins in the Empire Room are made.

FEBRUARY 1998

David Trimble is expected to make a hardline speech at a significant meeting of the Ulster Unionist Council executive to ward off a possible leadership challenge. Many fingers are crossed.

MARCH 1998

A highly confidential internal NIO document is leaked to unionists. The report, prepared by Tom Kelly, former BBC political correspondent and head of information at the NIO, details plans to secure a Yes vote in the proposed referendum by enlisting the help of non-political public figures such as Archbishop Robin Eames.

MARCH 1998

The Good Friday Agreement:
there were long hours and little
sleep for the negotiators.

APRIL 1998

The agreement reveals strange
bedfellows.

APRIL 1998

The first official meeting for
seventy-five years between a
unionist and a Sinn Féin leader
takes place largely due to outside
pressure.

SEPTEMBER 1998

At a Sinn Féin rally in the Ulster Hall it is revealed that the IRA has given a cautious welcome to the Good Friday Agreement but refuses to decommission. David Trimble reacts by holding a press conference at Glengall Street where he calls on Sinn Féin to accept both the 'gains and the pains' of the Stormont document.

MAY 1998

A parody of the government pro-agreement information broadsheet.

MAY 1998

The opening of the 108-strong power-sharing Northern Ireland Assembly is anything but dignified. An unseemly skirmish between the outgoing leader of the Alliance Party, John Alderdice, and his deputy leader, Seamus Close, over the position of initial presiding officer does great damage to the party's credibility.

JULY 1998

David Trimble comes under pressure from Union First, a new hardline action group including 'dinosaurs' Willie Ross and Willie Thompson and 'baby barristers' David Brewster and Peter Weir. The group, composed mainly of dissident UUP members, is strongly opposed to the Good Friday Agreement.

OCTOBER 1998

Former UUP leader James
Molyneaux pours scorn on the
Good Friday Agreement and the
Waterfront Hall U2 concert.

MAY 1998

With Bill Clinton's second
Northern Ireland visit fast
approaching, pressure mounts on
David Trimble to speak directly
to Sinn Féin.

SEPTEMBER 1998

OCTOBER 1998

The process that lifts David Trimble to Nobel heights was sweated over by countless unknowns.

OCTOBER 1998

After a frustrating trip to the North to kick-start a faltering peace process,
Tony Blair moves south and receives a hero's welcome. He is the first British
prime minister to address both houses of the Irish parliament.

NOVEMBER 1998

By attempting to deal with the less contentious issues of cross-border bodies and new government departments, Tony Blair and Seamus Mallon try to ease the UUP into a modest advance.

DECEMBER 1998

The risk of separating leaders from their parties.

DECEMBER 1998

34

A parody of a controversial Tory photo-montage showing Tony Blair and Mo Mowlam on Helmut Kohl's knees. This cartoon refers to the leaking of a secret Northern Ireland Office document indicating that a consensus of the secretary of state, the RUC chief constable and the chairman of the Parades Commission had agreed to let Orangemen walk the Garvaghy Road before ongoing negotiations were completed – 'the least worst option'. Mowlam denies that such a consensus has been reached, and the RUC claim to know nothing about it.

JULY 1997

Mo Mowlam accepts the LVF ceasefire. The organisation states that it is prepared to hand over a haul of weapons providing the IRA hands over ten times as much.

NOVEMBER 1998

MARCH 1999

NOVEMBER 1998

DECEMBER 1998

David Trimble's active relationship with Bertie Ahern and Adams's similarly productive meetings with Tony Blair appear somewhat bizarre.

FEBRUARY 1999

Secret talks between British government officials and Sinn Féin result in the latter being offered entry into all-party talks within six weeks of an IRA ceasefire. The secret deal is shattered days later with the murder of two RUC officers in Lurgan.

JUNE 1997

There! – we'll throw that nasty one away!

SEPTEMBER 1997

The Spice Girls kick off their world tour at the Point Depot in Dublin.

FEBRUARY 1998

As the Belfast Arts Theatre closes its doors for the last time, preparations are under way for the opening of the new political theatre at Stormont . . .

JANUARY 1999

38

NATO starts bombing the Serbs . . . The ironies of history sometimes lack subtlety.

MARCH 1999

Skeletons rattle in various cupboards.

FEBRUARY 1999

David Trimble is much more active in promoting his version of the spirit of the agreement (decommissioning) than Gerry Adams is in pushing his version of the letter (forming an executive). As a result Bertie Ahern appears to switch sides.

In America Lennox Lewis squares up to Evander Holyfield for the world heavyweight boxing championship.

MARCH 1999

David Trimble argues a triggering of d'Hondt will achieve nothing other than his political demise. Sinn Féin maintains that he has not tried to sell the agreement to his own supporters.

APRIL 1999

Government hints that talks' participants are poised to 'jump together' prove to be wishful thinking.

APRIL 1999

Raw sectarian invective hurled at David Trimble when entering Portadown town hall is recorded by television news crews, alienating many 'moderate' anti-agreement unionists and strengthening Trimble's negotiating hand. Similarly the horror of the Omagh bomb in August 1998 reduces extremist pressure on Adams.

MAY 1999

Mo Mowlam protests that her judgement of the state of the IRA ceasefire cannot be accredited to the much-quoted 'dogs on the street'.

AUGUST 1999

Ed Maloney, northern editor of the *Sunday Tribune*, is ordered by a crown court judge to hand over to the police notes of an interview he conducted in 1990 with William Stobie, the man charged in June 1999 with the murder of solicitor Pat Finucane in 1989. Moloney, one of the country's most respected investigative journalists, refuses to release his notes on the grounds that it would constitute a betrayal of journalistic ethics, and that in any case the police were already in possession of all the relevant information. Many observers wonder why, if this is true, the police have taken so long to act.

SEPTEMBER 1999

The historic role of the British in exiling petty offenders, as described in 'The Fields of Athenry', is taken on by the IRA. One awaits the ballads.

SEPTEMBER 1999

Following a summer of posturing and entrenchment, the UUP and Sinn Féin seem less than enthusiastic at renewing engagement at the review talks. Facilitator George Mitchell appears equally underwhelmed.

SEPTEMBER 1999

The United States and the Peace Process

Gerry Adams creates a media frenzy when he visits the US on a forty-eight-hour visa. A conference held in his honour at Manhattan's Waldorf-Astoria hotel is also attended by John Alderdice.

I've stolen most of the New Yorkers from various American cartoonists.

FEBRUARY 1994

The US administration grants a second visa to **Gerry Adams** – other visitors attract less attention.

SEPTEMBER 1994

48

Patrick Mayhew is adamant that Sinn Féin will not be admitted to a forthcoming
economic conference in Belfast. Two phone calls, one from the White House and the
other from the US ambassador in Dublin, produce an immediate U-turn.

DECEMBER 1994

Bill Clinton appears to have a roving eye for political as much as romantic liaisons.
The White House decision to invite Gerry Adams to the president's St Patrick's Day
reception is strongly criticised in Britain.

MARCH 1995

George Mitchell's saintly patience and skill are stretched to the limit.

NOVEMBER 1996

Guy waited three days at Drumcree Mr President! – Best get it over!

Sinn Féin have a direct link to the president – the UUP for the meantime has to settle for Vice-President Al Gore.

DECEMBER 1996

JULY 1998

The motorway is closed for Clinton's second visit.

SEPTEMBER 1998

The much-hyped destruction of LVF weapons is considered irrelevant to the decommissioning issue. Bill Clinton's instructions for the destruction of a so-called chemical weapons factory in Iraq are viewed as similarly diversionary.

DECEMBER 1998

The South

If a trip to the South used to feel like a journey back in time, it now seems as though, from a southern perspective, it is the North that is trapped in a time warp. With the financial sections of Dublin broadsheets as big as telephone directories, the North is seen by many southerners as little more than a historic sectarian folk park, suitable for property investment and not much else. Only Ballymena can still compete with Dublin for the title of drugs capital of Ireland.

It would be a big mistake, though, to assume that the South as a whole has turned its back on the North. Dick Spring and Albert Reynolds got a sharp reminder of this some years ago when they initially rejected John Hume's plea for support in his initiative to bring about a ceasefire by including Sinn Féin in the talks process.

The 'plain people of Ireland' showed them that the Celtic Tiger can roar about issues other than money, and the Fianna Fáil–Labour coalition was forced to perform the most acrobatic U-turn in recent Irish political history. A few years later the 'anyone but McAleese' campaign to block the northerner's chances of becoming Irish president foundered on the misconception that the South had turned partitionist. The British dimension, whether in agreement or disagreement, is here to stay and those who think differently are free to dress up and strut about their folk park.

DECEMBER 1993

Gerry Adams meets Proinsias de Rossa, the incoming Democratic Left leader in the South, at a meeting of the Forum for Peace and Reconciliation at Dublin Castle. Commentators are struck by the parallels in their careers.

DECEMBER 1994

John Taylor was the puppet master when this drawing went to press on the night the UUP was to choose its new leader. Two cut-out overlays, one of Ken Maginnis, and the other of David Trimble, were supplied in the event of an upset. Trimble's physique has never looked so beefy in subsequent cartoons.

SEPTEMBER 1995

Neil Jordan's interpretation of Michael Collins is hotly contested.

NOVEMBER 1996

Suspicion surrounds the two most newsworthy personalities of the moment. In the case of Michelle Smith, Ireland's Olympic heroine, there are rumours that she has used performance-enhancing drugs. For Charles Haughey, the scandal centres on the usual thing – money.

AUGUST 1997

Patrick Mayhew's announcement that he will not stand for re-election is overshadowed by Mary Robinson's declaration that she will not seek a second term as president.

MARCH 1997

Chancellor Gordon Brown puts four pence on a gallon of petrol causing a flood of northern drivers to head south to fill up.

MARCH 1998

A urine sample from Michelle Smith, Ireland's Olympic-swimming gold medallist, is found to have been spiked with alcohol.

JULY 1998

Spin doctor Eoghan Harris was the brain behind Mary Robinson's successful campaign for the Irish presidency in 1990. In 1997 his support for Irish presidential candidate Derek Nally proves as damaging as his opposition to Mary McAleese is helpful.

NOVEMBER 1997

Mary McAleese is installed in Áras an Uachtaráin where as president she becomes guardian of the Irish constitution. Speculation is rife that she and Bertie Ahern may reclaim Articles 2 and 3, previously offered as an unconditional gift to unionists by Mary Robinson and John Bruton.

NOVEMBER 1997

NOVEMBER 1997

In the face of mounting evidence of financial impropriety the Boss's instinct is to go down fighting.

DECEMBER 1997

Bertie shows his skill.

JANUARY 1998

Orangemen & Residents

Anyone travelling through Northern Ireland in the summer is liable to find the road blocked by Orangemen demonstrating their right to keep the roads open. They argue that their marches are traditional, that their behaviour is invariably restrained and – hey, you used to love all the music and colour before Sinn Féin told you that you didn't. However, in the nationalist areas through which these marches pass, residents object on the grounds that the marches are anti-Catholic, triumphalist and generally offensive. Dublin-born Ruth Dudley Edwards, the Orangemen's self-appointed spin doctor, insists that the Orangemen are simple souls, unskilled in the sophisticated arts of persuasion. Those on the receiving end of the marches feel that the Orange Order has become too used to imposing its will on others and simply sees no reason to explain itself.

The Parades Commission, meanwhile, attempts to strike an unhappy medium, operating under the impression that some kind of balance can be struck between lots of marches forced through Catholic areas and no Catholic marches forced through. Whatever the rights and wrongs of the situation, it is clear that as long as even a few Orange marches are actively forced through Catholic areas, Orangemen will get little public support outside the North.

Drumcree Two looms with no sign of any coherent strategy from the government.
An impression grows that government policy is determined by short-term expediency
and head counts rather than any discernible moral evaluation.

JULY 1996

As tension continues to build in Drumcree, the government gives in to Orange mob rule. Seldom has nationalist belief in the good faith of Westminster been more effectively demolished.

JULY 1996

Will we have to learn a second tune for the Arts Council?

The Arts Council of Northern Ireland awards a grant towards the study of Orange culture.

FEBRUARY 1997

I'm worried about peaking too early in the marching season.

FEBRUARY 1997

If music be the food of love . . .

AUGUST 1997

FEBRUARY 1997

It's their latest tactic –
TWEEDiation!

MAY 1997

Have you ever considered
appealing for a gentler, more
inclusive Harryville?

SEPTEMBER 1997

DECEMBER 1997

The only way to make him
exercise is to forbid him
from walking down the
Garvaghy Road!

JUNE 1997

The management is in a panic –
there's a rumour Drumcree
Three has been cancelled!

JUNE 1997

How dare you deprive
me of my culture!

JULY 1997

The well-known quotation – 'when I hear the word "culture", I reach for my gun' – from Hanns Johst, often attributed to Hermann Goering, strikes a chord with many who are gagging from force-feeding by an exclusive culture.

OCTOBER 1997

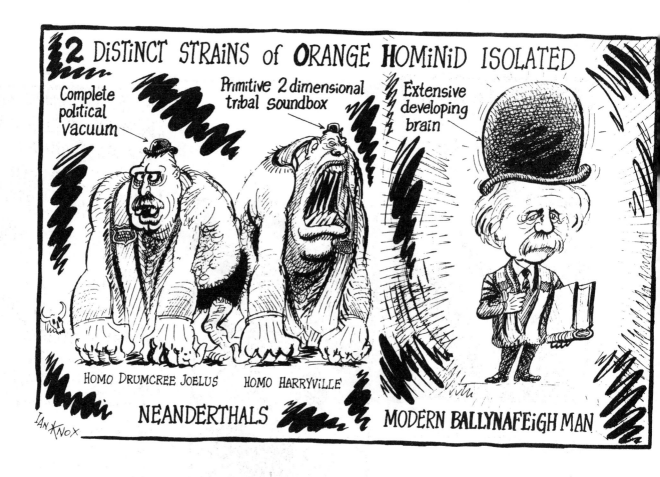

Doctor Svante Paabo of Munich University, after examining a DNA sample from a fossilised skull fragment, announces that Neanderthal man was not after all our ancestor.

When the Orange hierarchy calls off a controversial march down the lower Ormeau Road, Joel Patton, then chief spokesperson for the militant Spirit of Drumcree group, accuses the leadership of 'complete incompetency and cowardice'. Ian Paisley sees it as an act of betrayal which is comparable to the Munich Agreement of 1938.

JULY 1998

Tony Blair flies in to try to diffuse Drumcree tension.

JUNE 1998

Heat is generated at the mock battle at Scarva when appeals to end the Drumcree stand-off are countered by cries of 'traitor' and umbrellas are brandished.

JULY 1998

Pastor Kenny McClinton, who acts as a spokesperson for the LVF, was convicted of two murders in 1977. Breandán Mac Cionnaith, councillor and spokesperson for the Garvaghy Road residents, was associated with an attack on a British Legion hall in Portadown.

JULY 1998

When the Parades Commission announces that the Drumcree march will be re-routed away from the Garvaghy Road, the Orange Order defiantly proclaims that it will stay at Drumcree 'for as long as it takes' to get down that road. Arson attacks on ten Catholic churches are attributed to the LVF.

JULY 1998

In the interests of furthering mutual understanding, Mary McAleese invites Orangemen to stage a display in the grounds of Áras an Uachtaráin.

MARCH 1998

JUNE 1998

JULY 1998

JULY 1998

JULY 1998

JULY 1998

LOOK! — HE'S LEARNING TO MARCH !

AUGUST 1996

A report from the Northern Ireland Affairs Select Committee suggests that membership of organisations such as the loyal orders and the Ancient Order of Hibernians, 'who generally prohibit membership on religious grounds', is incompatible with membership of a public service organisation, 'especially the RUC'.

JULY 1998

Despite heckling from dissident unionists and Tories and continuing low-level paramilitary activity, Mo Mowlam continues to implement elements of the Good Friday Agreement through a miserable wet summer.

AUGUST 1998

Bits 'n' Pieces

The trouble with trying to bring some sort of order into a collection of cartoons is that you can only get so far. This section marks the end of that order.

A good friend of mine, an Englishman who has lived here for many years, once told me that the thing he liked least about Northern Ireland was what he called 'soda farl chauvinism'. He was referring, I think, to the way we tend to elevate folksiness into an art form – a kind of macho parochialism or inverted snobbery. I think there's probably a lot of truth in this.

The day after the declaration of a united Germany, Belfast's lord mayor, Fred Cobain, sets off on an unsuccessful mission to twin his divided city with Berlin.

OCTOBER 1990

Any remaining credibility the Police Authority may have enjoyed as an independent watchdog is effectively destroyed by the sacking of its chairman David Cook and his colleague Chris Ryder after a vote of no confidence in February.

MARCH 1996

Are these the infamous 'grey mists of an Irish Republic'?

Bad weather greets the royal visit to Northern Ireland.

JUNE 1997

I'M AFRAID MR. TRIMBLE REFUSES TO SPEAK TO FORMER TERRORISTS!

David Trimble attends a state banquet at Buckingham Palace in honour of Nelson Mandela despite advising Orangemen against meeting Breandán Mac Cionnaith.

JULY 1997

Speaking on BBC Radio Ulster's *Talkback*, upper Falls representative Alex Maskey states that as Sinn Féin lord mayor he would be perfectly prepared to carry out such onerous duties as toasting the queen.

JULY 1997

Prince Charles clearly enjoys his visit to 'non-British' Ireland. News that the Provos have dropped their 'exclusion order' on royalty leaves him underwhelmed.

APRIL 1995

The DHSS recommends the axing of acute services at the Whiteabbey and Mid-Ulster hospitals. Four new ambulances will carry emergency cases to Antrim, Belfast or the new Causeway hospital in Coleraine.

SEPTEMBER 1998

The DHSS sanctions pay rises for executives which are seen by many as excessive.

OCTOBER 1998

Accident and Emergency services in the South Tyrone hospital in Dungannon are to be cut.

JANUARY 1999

If you can't be neutral, try and be partisan in a more balanced kind of way.

On taking up the post of RUC chief constable, Ronnie Flanagan declines to ban membership of the loyal orders or masonic lodges for serving policemen. Admitting that he was once a mason, he cautions others that 'misconceptions can arise on the total neutrality of officers'.

NOVEMBER 1996

There is uproar surrounding the RUC/Donegall Celtic fixture as Sinn Féin puts pressure on Donegall Celtic to cancel the match. However, the subsequent euphoric cross-community support for the Ulster rugby team shakes the rigid boundaries of sports apartheid.

JANUARY 1999

The Christian Brothers express their 'deep regret' to anyone who has been ill-treated while in their care. A bizarre advertising blitz both north and south offers free phone counselling to those in need of help.

MARCH 1998

APRIL 1999

Well it was worth a try . . .

Chances of exploiting US presidential candidate Ross Perot's Ulster ancestry fade with Bill Clinton's re-election

NOVEMBER 1996

MARCH 1998

The poultry industry faces disaster after the seventh outbreak of the highly contagious Newcastle disease was confirmed.

FEBRUARY 1997

SEPTEMBER 1991

Unionisms

I've got a section here on unionist politics, but no equivalent one on nationalist politics, because, well . . . unionist politics are much funnier. You might feel that a group of people grimly opposed to change would be less amusing than another group who feel that history is on their side, but it doesn't seem to work like that. Aside from all the horrors of the last thirty-odd years – the slogans, the debates, the atrocities – it seems to me that while nationalism/republicanism might throw out more big ideas, unionism generates more jokes.

At the UUP annual conference, a speaker calls for the protection of schoolchildren against 'the promotion of the theory of evolution'. A map on the platform depicts Northern Ireland surrounded by water.

OCTOBER 1991

MAY 1993

Bob McCartney's victory in the North Down by-election of June 1995 precipitates a leadership crisis in the UUP.

JUNE 1995

Rumours of sleazy deals and accusations of betrayal of principle abound when the
Scott Report, investigating the selling of arms to Iraq, is debated in Westminster.
When the DUP actually saves the Tories from defeat, Mid-Ulster MP Willy McCrea puts
forward the amazing defence that it was not the right time to 'undermine the authority
of government'.

FEBRUARY 1996

A whispering campaign against moderate North Belfast UUP MP Cecil Walker by young
extreme right-wingers dominates the party's annual conference in Ballymena.
Revelations of Trimble's talks with LVF leader Billy Wright also prove embarrassing.

OCTOBER 1996

With his political demise imminent, John Major's one consolation is the prospect of release from the UUP balance-of-power stranglehold.

MARCH 1997

At a DUP/UKUP rally in Portadown, shrill denunciations of the UUP for 'giving up on the Union' are drowned out by news of an even shriller 'anyone but McAleese' smear campaign emanating from a southern clique.

OCTOBER 1997

The DUP's Sammy Wilson uses Billy Wright's name to inflame a crowd in Portadown.

MARCH 1998

**Of course I'm prepared to
fight my corner!**

Following the renewed IRA
ceasefire, David Trimble
talks tough on
decommissioning. Some
observers believe he is
looking over his shoulder at
his deputy.

JULY 1997

**So I said to Tony, either Mo
goes or I go!**

JANUARY 1998

SEPTEMBER 1998

I refuse to talk to Sinn Féin if they're linked to the IRA and I see no point in talking to them if they're not!

In an article in *An Phoblacht/ Republican News* the IRA distances itself from Sinn Féin's acceptance of the Mitchell Principles. Angry unionists are faced with an awkward dilemma.

SEPTEMBER 1997

NOVEMBER 1998

Using the protection of parliamentary privilege, Ian Paisley reads out a list of names he claims are IRA suspects leaked from secret RUC files. Those named protest their innocence and police deny the authenticity of the quoted source.

JANUARY 1999

APRIL 1998

The UKUP falls apart as Bob
McCartney's other four assembly
members desert him over his
insistence on withdrawal from the
assembly if Sinn Féin takes up
ministerial positions or if strong
cross-border bodies are established
prior to IRA decommissioning.

DECEMBER 1998

The impact of Conor Cruise
O'Brien's resignation from the
UKUP is largely overshadowed, at
least in Britain, by the Ron
Davies affair.

OCTOBER 1998

After an attempt by Tony Blair to allay unionist fears over the Good Friday Agreement, Jeffrey Donaldson and David Trimble issue contradictory statements.

MAY 1998

In the wake of the Nobel award, the pressure on David Trimble to make some gesture of accommodation towards Sinn Féin is eased by the IRA's negative stance on decommissioning.

DECEMBER 1998

Enraged at receiving a parking ticket while on government business, Ken Maginnis refuses to pay the fine and sends the ticket to Mo Mowlam.

FEBRUARY 1999

A bizarre meeting of Friends of the Union at Lord Cranborne's ancestral home,
Hatfield House, recalls previous liaisons between the extreme right and members of the
British establishment.

NOVEMBER 1998

Prisons & Paramilitaries

Those detained in the paramilitary wings of modern prisons exert great political power and control over events on the outside. This undisputed fact frightens, infuriates, puzzles and depresses those uninvolved in paramilitarism, but it remains a reality. Before the emergence of an articulate political loyalism, leaders of mainstream unionist parties were happy to court the hard men for their street credibility. However, the rise of the PUP and the UDP as vote winners has changed matters. Nowadays a unionist politician may frame an attack on one of the loyalist parties as a stalking horse for a non-sectarian-sounding attack on republicans. Those unionist parties that 'protest too much' about decommissioning, democrats and non-democrats, tend to have evolved from very non-democratic, very paramilitary origins. Genuinely non-violent parties tend to be pragmatic and inclusive though even the most compromising find their tolerance stretched by the early release issue. It is, however, worth bearing in mind Mo Mowlam's high-risk gamble of visiting the hardest men in their compounds, a move which saved the loyalist ceasefire and greatly reduced the casualty list. The road to peace, it seems, will be signposted by deals and horse trading rather than by comfortably sitting on our principles.

LONG CAGE

Two UDR men are killed by a bomb in Armagh. Four Catholic men are shot dead in a Cappagh pub. A Catholic taxi driver is shot dead in the Woodvale area of Belfast. A picket of the UDA headquarters by the New Consensus group – which includes Ken Maginnis and Reg Empey among its members – is attacked by Sammy Wilson, the DUP's press officer, and by Sinn Féin councillor, Gerard McGuigan.

AUGUST 1991

JANUARY 1993

SEPTEMBER 1993

After a series of beatings this weasel phrase is wearing very thin.

FEBRUARY 1997

What we want are pure Ulster tourists!

The LVF carries out arson attacks on tourist information offices in Banbridge and Newcastle as a protest against the promotion of cross-border tourism.

MARCH 1997

I'm just a Limestone Cowboy . . .

In Belfast loyalist gangs from Tiger's Bay indulge in an orgy of window-breaking on the Limestone Road.

APRIL 1997

Sorry about the queue, your excellency. Sinéad O'Connor and Liam Gallagher should be out shortly!

Anyone of any consequence visits the Maze prisoners.

JANUARY 1998

I'm not saying that the regime was too relaxed, but the latest tunnels started on the outstide!

MARCH 1998

LVF prisoners are excluded from the early release scheme.

JULY 1998

Visits by the UDP's Gary McMichael and mainstream politicians to loyalist prisoners in the Maze fail to influence the prisoners' decision to withdraw support for the talks. However, within hours of a visit by Mo Mowlam, they change their minds.

JANUARY 1998

Violence from republican dissidents threatens to bring about the expulsion of Sinn Féin from the talks.

FEBRUARY 1998

The Omagh bomb.

AUGUST 1998

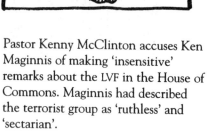

Support for republican violence had been draining away anyway. After Omagh it was all but gone.

AUGUST/ SEPTEMBER 1998

Pastor Kenny McClinton accuses Ken Maginnis of making 'insensitive' remarks about the LVF in the House of Commons. Maginnis had described the terrorist group as 'ruthless' and 'sectarian'.

NOVEMBER 1998

SEPTEMBER 1998